QUANTUM SPEAK

GOLDYN DUFFY

Printed in the United States of America First Printing, 2019
ISBN 978-0-578-46431-2

www.goldynduffy.com

Acknowledgements

Creating this book has been through a life time of some very cool and extreme experiences. I could not have written this or created an amazing life without the love of my life Michael Duffy. He has not only supported my journey in following my dreams but he has done everything possible to ensure that we live an incredibly abundant life. The feelings of appreciation I have for finding the love of my life so early and for continuing a journey of deepening love with someone who is so willing to live his greatest potential is what has empowered me to act on my gifts, talents and dreams and live the life we live today. His vibrational set point is always one of success and because of that he has once again created an amazing business out of his confidence, will and faith. We are a brilliant team and as a result have created some amazing women that make the Duffy tribe what it is. To each one of my gorgeous daughters Jade, Kaylee, Emma, and Shaelinn, who have taught me the truest meaning of unconditional love and what it means to be in relationship with strong women. And finally to my beautiful Kinsley Jane who has brought even more joy into our lives and made me a Gigi. It is through the love I feel with her that I have felt the cleanest love on earth.

I also could not have created this book without an incredible team of people who not only inspired me to keep going but made sure that I was always working from solution energy. To Diane DePreta who worked so hard to make sure that this book made sense and was grammatically correct. Her encouragement and determination for my information to present at it's greatest potential is why this book reads so well. To BJ whose alignment with my vision and solid connection to the material helped me to bring a lifetime dream to fruition. To Jess, my M21 partner and soul sister, who walked me through some of my old stories to help me heal what I needed to share my message with the world. And to my angel on earth Lisa Jones, who has spent endless hours talking to me and helping me to clarify the messages that have brought so many of my manifestations into physical form.

Contents

Introduction

You are pure positive energy that is connected to the stream of All That Is. You have access to Infinite Intelligence anytime you quiet your mind and invite your awareness of It in.

You are here to discover that you are an unlimited being with infinite potential and because you are reading this book, it is time for you to step fully into your truth.

Can you imagine what the world would be like if we all walked around with this knowing? If we all let go of unworthiness and our beliefs about lack and limitation? If we all stepped off the merry go round and stopped making a big deal about the shit that just doesn't matter and instead started living from our greatest potential. That's the world I'm interested in. That's the reason I am writing this book and sitting outside on a beautiful Southern California day and telling you that it is possible. Not only is it possible but the tides are already turning in your favor as you take all of this in. As we awaken the truth within, we activate all that is possible in this unlimited adventure called life.

You may be wondering how Quantum Physics, which is the study of photons, electrons and other particles that make up the universe, have anything to do with creating your life. This is a simple guide to help you see the relationship between your thoughts, feelings and beliefs and how they are conducting the energy that is creating your world. It has been shown that Quantum Physics is related to consciousness. Our brains are a physical organism that transmit electrochemical signals. These signals are directly related to the behaviors of molecules and atoms that dictates what is created in the physical world.

When you enlighten yourself to the knowledge of how your brain sends out the waves that create your reality, you begin to live life from a very different perspective. We begin to ignite the fire within our own creating power and discover our limitless nature. Life begins to be a fun, interactive, expansive and miraculous journey, where we get to contribute deliberately in what we experience.

This doesn't have to be complicated. There are very simple laws in the Universe that apply to our everyday experiences. Once we know the laws and get really good at understanding them, we gain access to the most powerful energy in the Universe.

Everything is energy. There is a vibratory force that is conducted by each one of us and the things that make up our world. When I refer to your vibration I am referring to your state. How you are thinking and feeling; your mood. We all know what it feels like when we meet someone who is light and fun. We also know what it's like when we meet someone who is heavy and low. These moods that we encounter conduct a vibration that then tune us into a frequency of like vibrations. So when we are feeling really light and happy, we will meet others and experiences that match that happy, light vibration. When we are frustrated or in a bad mood, we will tune ourselves into a frequency with more things that are a match to that. Flat tires, spilled coffee, head colds, car accidents and the other annoying things live on this vibrational plane.

This journey is ours to create. If you have been living as a victim up until now, it is time to let that go. It's time to take back your power. Let go of limiting belief systems and use the power of science and spirituality to ignite the true gifts, talents and joy you are capable of.

One of my favorite books on this subject is Do You QuantumThink by Dianne Collins. She enlightens readers to the idea of a "new world order." Her assistance in making us all wake up and become one of the leading edge changemakers is extremely powerful and inspiring. Here she explains what it is like to live life from a QuantumThink perspective.

"You transcend your limited experience of time and go from overwhelm to relaxed alertness. You are comfortable with change because that is the nature of life. Instead of resisting or merely "embracing" change, you actively work with it. You use change to your benefit. You are no longer daunted by uncertainty; in fact, you appreciate it, knowing that it is only because of things not being firmly in cement for all time that you and I can fashion ourselves and our circumstances anew."

It's time to educate ourselves about the energetic world and stop believing that what has already been created is all there is. Your life is a creation of your past thoughts, so what's happening is actually old news. There is so much more to be experienced and it is time for us all to wake up and start creating.

Quantum Speak

We can take this life very seriously, fussing and struggling all the time just trying to make life work. We spend way too much time worrying about things that never happen and living like we are in survival mode on a consistent basis. Over the span of our life, we have formed belief systems that have created lack and limitation, and most likely we are not even aware of them. However, many of us are on a path now where we are starting to wake up. We are starting to realize that there is a better way to live and we must find it.

If this is you, great job! You are on your way to introducing new belief systems that will help you to become a deliberate creator in your life.

This book is here to lead you to living a better life. It is here to help you form the knowing of your power and very clear instructions on how to conduct energy in your favor. For most of our lives, we have lived by default, feeling as though life is pushing us around and that we are not in charge of anything.

We may have grown up believing that we really don't have any control over anything. That all we can do is pray and hope for the best. We see "bad" things happen to good people all the time and we can walk around with an impending feeling of doom, unless we educate ourselves to another way.

As we grow older, I believe the foundations of all we have been taught about life may not work anymore. If we are working on ourselves and expanding from the Universal information that is coming forth, we begin to find a whole new way to live. When you start to question the programmings you have been brought up with or the meaning of life at all, you quickly realize that there has to be more.

There are a million teachings out there, so how are we to know which one is the truth? The only way we can really know is by what we are experiencing in our lives. If you prayed really hard for something as a kid, like I did (it was a baby doll), and you didn't get it, you may have formed the belief that God does not exist or that He doesn't ever give you what you want. If you prayed for a relative to get better after receiving a terminal illness diagnosis and they still died, well you get my point.

These experiences stay with us. They form belief systems around our lives and then they create exactly what we believe.

For those of you out there that believe you are unlucky and shit always happens to you, I can assure you that this is a product of a deeper belief system that you have been perpetuating your entire life. That is why you keep seeing evidence of it. Even when something really good happens you say things like, "Well I'm just waiting for something to go wrong because this is just too good to be true." And then of course something goes wrong!! You decided that!

I believe that the the vast amount of information we have been enamored with has caused us to become slightly confused. We look at people's social media performances and wonder how in the world everyone could be doing so well, when our lives are a fragment of what we want them to be.

I'm going to tell you right here and now, no one knows what the hell they're doing! And the more people try to convince you that they do, and then charge you a lot of money to give you information that you already have inside of you, the more they are full of shit.

The reason I believe this book is valuable to you is because it will lead you to the truth you possess inside. It will help you clear out all of the jargon and the false belief systems you have lived with up until now and help you gain a clarity that will assist you in creating the life you have always wanted.

Quantum leaping is for those who are serious, who have decided that they have the ability to focus and they no longer want to play victim in their lives. If you are one to make excuses or don't want to take on the awesome responsibility of reality creation, you can stop reading this right now. I have a feeling though, if you picked this book up, that your curiosity and burning desire to become the deliberate creator you were born to be may just keep you with me.

1

STOP DOING AND START BEING

Ok so right now I want you to STOP. Yes, stop reading, take several deep breaths and feel your body from your head to your toes. Go on, just do it. Take stock of your body and all the little tensions and things you have been ignoring. Breathe deeply and bring yourself fully into this moment.

This is what I mean when throughout the book, I ask you to drop into your body.

The mind is a tricky character and it will often try to derail us in an effort to keep us from growing. The mind is always here to keep us safe and by doing anything outside of our comfort zone, it must always kick up a fight and try to distract us. When you take deep breaths and drop into your body, you will allow your mind to quiet. This gives you space to make new decisions, create new energies and see new possibilities forming because of your shift from the mind to the creative center that lives within you.

Your very first assignment in reality creation is going to be to practice quieting your mind. You cannot create something different until you get the mind to shut up about what it's been saying to you over and over again, all day long. In order to create new energies and new outcomes we must first get away from the thought patterns that have driven your reality up until now. Quieting your mind is the way. In Quantum Physics this is called "Zero State Awareness." It is the starting place of creation energy and it is the where all of your power exists.

Now I can go on and on about the benefits of this type of practice but knowing that you have Google at your fingertips and I promised you a quick guide, I will spare you. I will say this, the practice of quieting your mind is the single most important thing you can do in becoming a deliberate creator.

If you would like help in quieting your mind, subscribe to the M21 Revolution, an online meditation and mindful program with guided practices and leading edge information on universal law. www.goldyn-duffy.com/m21-revolution

2

POWER IN CLARITY

So whether you have realized a desire recently or it has been a desire you have had for a long, long time, the process is pretty much the same. Concerning the things that you have been wanting for a long time, you may need to work a little more in unleashing the beliefs that have kept it from you. With newer desires, you may have to exercise a little patience, as it takes some time for the physical world to catch up with the energetic world.

I have spoken with many people that want to leave their jobs and as soon as they start voicing that out loud, their job just seems to get worse and worse. I like to call that "nails in the coffin". It is giving your desire a greater opportunity to become stronger.

A great way to look at situations like that is, sometimes it has to get really bad or be completely taken away from us before we will do anything about it. Sometimes, the Universe has to force us out, or make it so intolerable that we take the leap of faith we need to take for things to get better.

Ok so drop into your body before you read any further. Come on…. deep breaths… feel the present moment and allow your mind to clear. Just a few deep breaths will do wonders for your creative powers. It will also help you to get in a mode of receiving to allow you to ingest what I am dishing out. That last paragraph got you thinking way too much and we need to have a quiet mind to get into this next part.

Becoming clear on what you want in great detail is a really good way to manifest what you want. By focusing clearly, seeing, feeling and experiencing in your mind what you are looking to create, you are painting the picture and aligning your energetic output with the resonance of all that you are wanting.

Ok that was a lot to take in. Just breathe. Clarity is about activation. As we become clear we begin to create. It's like you are sending a letter to the Universe saying this is what I want and I want it in this color.

This may go against the beliefs that you were given as a child that said, "Take what you get and don't get upset." Right, like being picky meant we were spoiled and having preferences was wrong. I challenge you to let this belief system go. Right now. How do you do that?

Breathe, deeply. Ask that this belief system that has made you feel powerless to what you receive in life leave you, now. Done. Boom. Seem easy? It is. Moving forward you need to become super aware of the patterns and habits of thought that keep that belief alive. As you become aware you can let go and create from a new energy.

Great things to say to interrupt patterns are:

~That is not true for me anymore
~I believe in my ability to create something different

~I know I have the power to create

You must interrupt the old mental patterns in order to create something new. We have 60,000 thoughts per day and about 90 percent of them are the same thoughts we had yesterday. It's time to take more of your creative control back.

Whatever it is that you desire, begin by writing it down. Get super detailed and feel into the energy of each detail you list. See it as if, and feel it as if, you are already living it. It's time for you to fully identify with what you want in the energetic world. Manifesting and deliberate creation is so much easier when you start here. Writing is the strongest form of focus so get off your butt and go get a pen. I'll even give you a blank page to write on.

I'm serious. Do it. Right now. Write down exactly what you want and spend time feeling what it feels like. This is like putting in your order with the Universe and expecting it to be delivered. Spend time visualizing, seeing yourself from inside the visualization not outside of it. Instead, practice seeing through the eyes of yourself in the visualization. Look down at the clothes you are wearing and see the smile on your face in the mirror. See through the windshield of the car you wish to drive and see the scenery outside of your window.

Visualize with as much feeling and detail as you possibly can. This is what begins to formulate the energy and create from your partnership with the Universe. Ask yourself what it truly feels like to be the person you are envisioning. See if you can feel, act or dress from that new identity's point of view.

Write it down so you can gain clarity, feeling and focus!!

Writing is the strongest form of focus

WRITE IT DOWN!

FEEL IT!

MANIFESTATION STORY

It's time to get really clear on what you want. It's time to create from a place of total intention and decision. It's time to see it and feel it as if it already has happened.

First, take some deep breaths. Come into a place of receiving and then read this story. Allow your spirit to receive it in a nonjudgmental, open to new possibilities sort of way.

These are different stories that I have used to create amazing things in my life. I include my manifestation stories to provide you with evidence of deliberate creating. We ALL have this ability and if you have not been using Universal Law to your fullest potential, my stories may help you believe until you do.

My Mercedes

So my love for Mercedes started about 7 years ago, when a nice gentleman asked me if I would drive his brand new 300E Mercedes home from the airport. He told me to "Drive it like I stole it!" I was allowed to drive the car all week until he came back from vacation. This car was amazing. It was the smoothest ride I have ever had and gave a whole new meaning to hugging the road. I fell madly in love with the car but felt no possibility of financially being able to have one, at that time. I created such a belief system around not being able to afford one and not having good enough credit that I purchased a used Infiniti for about the same price of a new Mercedes. Looking back now, I can see the limitations of my beliefs and how they kept me from enjoying the car of my dreams for longer. Fast forward, I moved to California with my Infinity and realized that I was deeply upside down in my loan for this car because I was desperate to make a deal and get a car at the time. I made some poor decisions when purchasing this car because I was operating from survival mode and desperation. All part of my learning process.

When I moved to California, I started to think about what I would want to trade my car in for and even went to a BMW dealership (at this point I forgot about my love for Mercedes and the ability to own one) to see if I could make the numbers work and trade in my perfectly fine car that had way too much negative equity in it. No dice. It kept coming up that I would need at least $7000 to trade in my car. Since we just made this giant leap across the country, our financial picture did not support a purchase like that. So I released it. Whenever I am feeling like something is difficult, I release it and love what I have, to allow for the energies to line up.

Appreciating what you have is a really good foundation to come from when you are looking to create something else. If we are unhappy and miserable with what is, we are conducting from a place of lack and will have no power over creating what we desire. Things don't manifest from the low vibrational state of misery. They manifest from the higher states like love, appreciation and joy.

I began putting my focus on different cars. Not really knowing what I wanted and always believing that a Mercedes was out of reach. After about two years, I became frustrated that my new car wasn't manifesting. I mean, here I am a manifestation expert and I couldn't see where I was blocking my own desire.

As business and finances improved, I began to get more serious about trading in my car. The mileage was getting high and I was feeling intuitively that it was time to create something new. I wanted something I felt really good in and that had a car payment which was similar to the car I was driving.

So, I took this information to my practice of quieting my mind. I asked deep down if I could have any car I wanted what it would be. I asked the question expecting to get the answer, then I let it go.

When you give your desires time, you allow the Universe to co-create with you. Every manifestation needs time to align with the physical energy. Every quantum wave we send out needs time to break down into particles and become matter. When we are impatient, we slow down the energy. When we are in positive expectation, we speed up the energy.

A few days later, I was driving around and saw a 2018 Mercedes GL350. My entire body lit up. I felt a hell yes! I could feel the connection of the energy of what I had been getting clear about. It was like I knew with every fiber of my being that this was my car. I even went to a dealership and test drove one. I fell completely head over heels in love. When I went into the dealership to see how much I would need to drive it, I still had the feeling that I was not going to be able to afford it. Yet. This was right before Christmas and after learning that I would need $5000 to drive this beautiful new car, I felt it was getting closer to my reality. The only thing I had to do was manifest the money, I've been known to manifest $10,000 so that didn't feel too far out of reach for me.

A few more months passed and it felt like nothing was happening. I started to get frustrated again and switched cars. I started feeling like the car that I really wanted was too far out of reach if it wasn't manifesting. I pulled my wave of desire away from the new car and continued to feel appreciative and grateful for the car that I was driving.

Then something miraculous happened, I started listening to the book by Frederick Dodson, "Parallel Universes of Self." In his book, he described how the reason we don't manifest something is because we are always changing what we want. He even cited an example and said, "The reason you don't manifest the car you want to drive is because you are not being clear and focused on a particular car." I felt like he was talking directly to me.

Around this time my friend Lisa came to visit. I told her about my car and that I was working on manifesting $5000. Lisa, who is an incredible manifestor and intuitive said, "I just don't feel like your going to need $5000." She said she could see it happening another way.

At this point, I could feel myself opening my mind to possibilities. I started to feel more hopeful and that the Universe was giving me messages that I was blocking by feeling it had to come in a certain way. So for two weeks I practiced. In his book, Fred told me to not visualize myself in the car but to visualize myself as if I was driving the car. I asked myself, "how would I feel if I drove by this car and I was already driving one?" I wouldn't be super excited or feel any kind of lack, I would just be nonchalant and say, "there's my car." I saw myself looking through the windshield and felt how I would feel when I saw it sitting in my driveway. Every day I would go for a jog at the bike trail, I would see the keys in my hand and imagine myself walking towards it when I was done with my run.

I then felt the inspiration to act. I decided that I would call a different dealership and talk to a salesperson about how much money I would need. My intention was to ask if it was better to pay $5000 (I was still stuck on that number) directly to my loan or bring it in with me. At this point, I knew it was happening but I still believed it would come with the $5000 manifestation. I was feeling very confident that I was going to manifest the money and buy the car.

The salesperson ended up being very cool, and fun. We had instant rapport on the phone and he talked me into coming in on Friday to take a look and see if we could make it work. I had received some other information from the Universe, while talking to some friends, that the best time to strike a deal is on the last day of the month. Friday was the day before the month closed. So I took that as another sign.

The next sign that came was when I called my current loan company on my current car. I found out that I was not as upside down as I had been thinking because I had been paying my loan for the last 7 months since looking at that first car. The amount owed had gone down considerably. I could feel movement in the energy with this information. When you start to see evidence of energy moving and flowing you know you are on to something and it's important to continue to follow the clues.

So on Friday, I went to the car dealership and met up with my car salesperson. We had a great time and started the negotiation process. During our time together, he couldn't seem to find the car I really wanted. I was being super specific because I know how energy works and I knew I didn't have to settle. He found a similar model that had a black interior and I wanted a light interior. He began negotiating and telling me I needed $3000 to get in this car. It was looking better. I called my husband, he said no way and hung up. I could feel the energy becoming frenetic as I was trying to make this happen for the car that I wasn't truly in love with. So I left. I told the car salesman that miracles happen all the time and I was willing to wait until my exact car showed up.

When we allow space for our manifestations to become easy and show us the signs that they are meant to be, we create from our power. When we get too attached to something and "try" very hard to "make" it happen, we activate desperate energy. When we are acting from this type of energy we are not in the allowing or receiving mode of life. We are no longer co-creating with our partner the Universe and the energy will get really thick and yucky.

The next morning he called me and said he found the exact car I was looking for. Of course he did. He then offered me a deal I knew was going to work. He said if I could come up with $2500 as a deposit, he could get me into the car payment I wanted. I then received a payment from one of my clients that morning, which brought me only $500 away from driving this car I had wanted for so long. I called my husband to give him the good news and he was still not feeling it. He said, "You told me you would be able to take care of the deposit and you don't have the money yet." You see, I promised him I would take care of the deposit and I wouldn't buy the car until I had the money.

In our marriage, if we both don't agree on something, then it's not right.

It was at that moment that things began to feel difficult, I felt like I was forcing it and I needed to let go. We rarely fight about anything and because we are so in tune, I knew if he wasn't feeling right about it, that I needed to back away from it. When he came home a few hours later I told him I was letting it go and he said, "I don't care what you do." Whoa, a shift in the energy. Five minutes later my incredible friend and angel, Lisa, sent over $500 to my PayPal. At that moment, I felt total elation and like the stars had aligned. I could feel the energy getting super light and supportive and feel the ease and flow that is available to us when we are in alignment. I later went to pick up my beautiful new car and felt so much gratitude for the journey. Oh and I forgot to mention, my car salesperson's name was Richard Wright. Mr. Wright. Seriously, you can't make this shit up.

After looking back over this experience, I am fully aware of when energy begins to feel difficult, and when I am trying to make things happen on my own agenda. When we do this, we cut the Universe out of our co-creative partnership. As soon as I let go and decided that it had to be easier, the energy shifted and support began to show up. Pay attention to the energy. Tune into how it feels. When it begins to flow and feel easy, that's when you know you are on the right path.

If there's a lot of frenetic energy or roadblocks that keep showing up that make it feel difficult, it's best to take a few steps back and let the situation breathe. I have found this usually means the original deal was not meant to be and there is something better waiting for me to release the hold on it. If there are people involved who are pressuring you, please know that if it is meant to be, nothing will stop it from happening. We have to stop doing things out of fear and start allowing the ease and flow of the Universe, because things often will work out better than we planned.

3

BELIEVE IT SO YOU CAN SEE IT

Great job on being super clear about your desire. If you are having issues believing in your ability to create big life changes, then I highly suggest you do this with something small. The Universe doesn't actually know the difference between big and small but our resistance around the big stuff can make it feel slower to come. So start with something small, decide that you will see something today.

Start with a butterfly, or a feather, or a yellow raincoat. It can be something you don't normally see, and then notice how many times you see it, when you decide to focus your attention. Our focus activates energy in our lives and as we intend to see something, we don't simply attract it, we actually create the energy within us to become more aware of it which then brings it into our experience.

We break down the quantum waves of energy and assist them in forming into the particles of the butterfly, the feather or the raincoat just by our energetic attention and intention to see them. We heighten our awareness and actually create matter in our field.

We are incredibly powerful beings and our focus is what activates energy into the alignment of creation. Once you show yourself how easy it is, I would challenge you to keep going with the manifestations you believe to be a bigger challenge.

Check in with your beliefs about where you are right now. It's really important to take total responsibility in where you are right now. The reason for this is because if you are living in denial of your own limiting belief systems, you will have trouble moving forward in manifesting your desires. I had to look at my belief around owning a Mercedes and step into the true worthiness and acknowledgment that I could strike a deal and drive one. I also had to believe in the co-creating powers of the Universe to support me in bringing my desires into the physical form.

Once you look at your beliefs, then decide which ones may be limiting. Look at which ones are holding you back from how you truly want to be living. Drop into your body, take some deep breaths and ask for these belief systems to be released from you.

Draw upon Divine Energy to give you higher vibrational perspectives about your desire. By asking for this transformation in the energy, you are inviting in the energy of All That Is. Some call it God, Source, Universe.

I really like to think of this as an Energy that is expressing through us that is interested in our activating the power we have access to. This is a co-creative partnership. You no longer have to go this journey alone! We have access to Infinite power and wisdom. The only thing we need to do is invite it in and have faith that all things are always working out for our highest and best.

Once you activate the faith, then call in and invite in the Infinite Power. Allow yourself to feel the excitement of what is about to transpire and then allow your desire to manifest. This means to let it go, release it and know that it is coming. Since we don't know how and we don't know when, it's best to keep ourselves in a place of feeling satisfied.

4

ALIGNING YOURSELF VIBRATIONALLY

This doesn't mean we sit around and wait. Waiting for something to happen is actually conducting the energy of waiting and will only slow energy down. This is the time to relax into the allowing energy and look for the signs and clues to act. It is time to be aware of what is going on in your experience, and work on releasing any impatient thoughts or feelings that make you feel like it's not happening fast enough. Start visualizing and aligning yourself with the energetic pre-quantum wave conduction.

Start asking yourself what this new identity looks and feels like.

Start doing things that help create the new identity around the person who is living your desired existence right now.

So everything you want has the ability to manifest because of your desire for it. Nothing happens until we form the thought patterns and desires to begin activating the energy of existence. **The fact that you have the vision and desire means you have what it takes to manifest it.** Realize that the journey to the manifestation is actually more important than the actual manifestation and you are halfway there. Understand that forming your energy around what you want is a necessary step in allowing it into your experience.

The feeling is the manifestation.

In order for things to manifest that we become focused on, we need to create the quantum wave of desire. Once we send out the wave of desire, the energy will then be conducted according to what we do next. If we begin doubting what we want to do or feel fearful, we allow our minds to give us lots of reasons why we can't do or have what we want. This will then interrupt the wave from becoming physical matter in our experience.

If we continue to believe, know and feel excited about our desires, following our intuition and feeling into what it feels like to have what we have asked for, we will catapult the wave and cause a quantum leap in energy.

I believe this is what happens to aspiring actors who are working so hard towards their dreams and then one day they get invited on the Tonight Show and their lives are never the same. It happens just like that and for some it may look like they got famous overnight but the reality is they have been aligning and sending out the wave of stardom for as long as it took for that overnight success to happen.

It's funny to think of people like Jerry Seinfeld working in dirty night clubs before he was discovered or Carly Simon singing in little bars terrified of her own gifts, because we have only known them as the legends we see today.

When you look at Carly Simon's story, you see a woman who was brought up being passionate about music but absolutely terrified of her talent. So terrified that she acquired a stutter and battled for years to speak correctly. You can see that her talent overtook her fear and she was able to share her talents with the world despite that fear. She was fearful and passed out on stage and **she did it anyway.** The journey was more important to her than her fear and she knew as she kept writing and singing and performing that it was what she was born to do.

I think that's the difference between those who have so called "made it" and those who are still questioning if they have what it takes. **They acted despite** their fear and anything else that got in their way, they just simply kept going.

Ok, so back to feeling into your manifestation. You may be asking at this point how in the world you can feel what it feels like if you've never experienced the manifestation before. This is where Divine Energy comes into play. It's time for you to recognize that you are an expression of Divine Energy, that you are here to allow life to be called through you, so you can share the Divine Light that is pulsing within.

Let's stop here and breathe, getting back into our bodies. Quiet your mind, take long slow deep breaths and invite in the Divine Infinite Wisdom to share with you what it feels like to vibrationally connect with what you have a strong desire for in your life. Allow your mind to give you the scenes, like a movie, of what your life is like **as** that new identity. Allow your visions to come to life inside that quiet space in your mind and feel the energetic resonance with the vision.
See yourself as that person looking out into the world from your manifested identitys' eyes. Allow yourself to feel the excitement, relief, and personality of this future self who is becoming in every moment you allow it to be. You must become this new identity in order to vibrationally resonate with the vision.

If you would like help in quieting your mind, subscribe to the M21 Revolution, an online meditation and mindful program with guided practices on identity creation. www.goldynduffy.com/m21-revolution

5

BECOMING A NEW IDENTITY

Recently I realized that I was on a rollercoaster with my weight. I would try all sorts of diets and exercise plans and lose the weight and feel good, then fall back into old habits and patterns that made me feel awful. I was frustrated and disgusted. I knew there had to be a better way. After meditating on this dilemma, I realized that the energy I had been conducting was that I was standing in a place of not knowing. Telling myself I didn't know what to eat or what to do to end this cycle. I decided to begin the process of identity creation with this situation and the results astounded me.

First I had to look at the beliefs I had created that got me where I was.

I could see that I had a belief that I was getting older and it was harder to lose weight in my 40s.

I couldn't work out because I didn't have a gym membership. I didn't have the motivation or consistency.

I didn't know what to eat.

I couldn't find anything long lasting that I could remain passionate about and create a lifestyle change with.

I began to create the mindset around the new identity that I wanted by meditating and becoming clear on what I wanted.

I started asking myself, "what would a person who has the body I want eat?" Soon after I manifested a nutrition plan that has been long lasting and has become a lifestyle change for me that I can attain.

Next I asked myself, "What would a person who has the body I want do?" Soon after, my husband came home with home gym equipment and I discovered a woman on Facebook who told me exactly what to do.

I became accountable to my new identity. There was no more excuses of not feeling like exercising or eating like crap. I no longer questioned if I was going to go for a run in the morning. I just did it.

I bought a scale. I have forever had a fear of scales and a belief that it never said what I wanted it to say. I made peace with the scale and realized that denial was not getting me closer to my goals. I weighed myself almost every day and stayed accountable by accepting the number as my indicator of what was working.

I became excited for this new identity and made a definite decision that this is who I am now.

I am happy to report that at 46 years old, I am in the best shape of my life. I feel amazing and strong. I have stepped into the identity that has helped me to release low level belief systems and mental anguish that I no longer encounter.

All of this came because I decided to be the girl that I feel the very best identifying with.

Stop trying to **do** something and **be** something instead.

IDENTITY CREATION

First, ask yourself and get super honest with where you are on the subject that you are looking to shift. It's important to get super clear about the beliefs and thoughts that have been creating what you do not want. Once you see them, you can begin interrupting them. If you can't see them, you have no power to change them.

Then create beliefs and thought patterns around what you want to create.

MAKE THE DECISION TO ACT FROM THIS NEW IDENTITY

It is so important to make the decision. If you don't decide, the Universe has only wishy-washy energy to work with. You have to decide who you want to be in order to activate the Universe in a quantum response.

Remember, the Universe is responding to your energetic output. It is not just what you are saying but how you are behaving and believing. This is why mantras don't always work because if you are saying them without feeling or belief, they're just empty words with no quantum energy behind them.

Body

If it is health you are looking for:

What would a person in a good feeling body do? What would they eat?

What thoughts would they think when they looked in the mirror?

What activities would they take part in if they lived in a good feeling body?

Would they ask questions like "Should I exercise today?" or "Should I eat that cookie?"

No. They would do what a person who was healthy and feeling good would do. They would not allow the tricky mind that wants to keep them from changing to call the shots anymore. They would no longer unconsciously reach for foods that do not serve their higher intention. They would instead become conscious to the energy that is creating their physical body and eat the high vibrational foods that will conduct their new identity into reality.

Finances

How would you feel if your finances were exactly how you wanted them to be?

How would you dress and where would you go?

How would you feel spending money if you had an abundance of money to spend?

How would you talk about things, would you mention how expensive things are or feel frustration over your bills?

If your desire is to have an abundance of money in this lifetime, it's time for you to start feeling abundant. Understand that the feeling is the manifestation and until you feel abundant you cannot possibly line up with those things that are abundant.

Would you feel stress or worry if you were at the financial place that you most want to be?

With finances, you may have to take your eyes off of the money and get into the vibrational place of abundance without looking at your bank account. Know that the bank account you are experiencing right now is only because of the thoughts and feelings you have had up until now. Our financial experiences can change very quickly when we put ourselves in vibrational resonance with abundance. What makes you feel abundant? Can you notice the abundant flowers, trees, sunshine or love in your life? Can you go places that make you see the abundance of the world we live in? There is no lack in this Universe and as soon as you start looking for reasons to feel abundant, the Universe will show you even more.

You can do this exercise with anything you are looking to step into. Asking yourself how the person who has what you want behaves, is one of the best ways to line yourself up with the energy. Inviting in Divine Energy to assist you in letting go of fears, and allow you to heal into the abundance that is your birthright, is an excellent practice to send you on your way.

I have tons of manifestation stories about finances. I have lived through many abundant times and many financial hardships. It wasn't until I got really clear and could see that the hardships were leading me to more faith and trust in my Universal support that I was able to truly step away. I found a way to be happy and joyful and to see this financial stuff as a game that I got to play. I knew that as I stepped more into my knowing, the more evidence I would see of my support. I knew that it was my living on the edge and experiencing uncertainty that was increasing my faith. I know now that without those opportunities that helped me create stronger desire, I would not have created the awareness and the healing that needed to take place in order for me to truly live in abundance.

If circumstances around your financial situation do not feel good right now, know that they are about to change. Once you understand that money is an energy, you can start as soon as now in creating an energetic output of abundance.

MANIFESTATION STORY

My favorite manifestation story came right after we moved across the country from Connecticut to California. We moved without having jobs or a place to live with two of our four daughters and our two cats. This was the bravest and craziest thing we had ever done. When we managed to manifest a great place to live and a job for my husband, the money wasn't quite covering everything we needed to cover. We got really good at playing the game of paying most of our bills, and feeling good during the experience. Our faith was upleveling exponentially and it all made perfect sense in our personal growth journey.

Not to say that we didn't experience boatloads of fear or worry, we just kept bringing ourselves back to our knowing and then kept receiving evidence of our support.

One night I went to Trader Joe's with $40 in my bank account. I was feeling really good and decided that I could spend that $40 on shrimp and langostinos! I knew that I lived in an abundant Universe and that the way I was feeling would create more. I left the store feeling great. Keep in mind, there was no more money in my bank account and **I still felt great.**

As I was walking out of the store I looked down on the ground and found a $100 bill. I swear! I looked up and thanked God and knew that everything was going to be ok. When I got home and told my husband he said, "We have nothing to worry about."

I have a million of these types of stories. Where we would have no money at the beginning of the day and by the end of the day there would be a random check in our mailbox. We practiced the art of feeling abundant every day and we never let fear get the best of us. Our confidence and faith continued to grow and gain strength and as a result our situation began to get better and better. In fact, in the short time of two years we ended up creating an incredible life of abundance with thriving businesses, a gorgeous home, a brand new car and many other evidences of our vibrational resonance with abundance.

6

ALLOWING AND RESISTANCE

Paying attention to how you feel is of the utmost importance when you are working with energetic alignment. If you are feeling stressed, frenetic, and desperate, it is a clear sign that you are not working in the co-creative partnership you have access to with the Universe. We have been brought up with the social programming that "if it's to be it's up to me." With that attitude, we block all of the Universal support that is trying to come to us. When we relax, quiet our minds and get back into alignment with Universal forces, we connect with the ease and flow of how life really works.

If you are currently involved with something that feels very difficult, it is because you have not engaged with the flow of the Universal support or you are trying to make something happen that is not in your highest and best interest.

This happens when we get too attached to certain outcomes and block ourselves off from the miracles. We introduce resistance every time we don't trust or expect that things are working out for us. Divine Energy would like to deliver something that is even better than we are allowing. When we are acting out of desperation or trying really hard to make something happen we are creating all sorts of energetic waves that go against the ease and flow of the natural order. Life is not supposed to be hard. Life is here to create joy and when we are in tune with the ease and flow, joy is much more easily accessed.

Now drop into your body, take some nice deep breaths and repeat the words "Life is meant to be easy." Again. "Life is meant to be easy." Keep this as a mantra to override the "Life is hard" old belief that it is time to let go of.

Anytime you are fighting against something, you are in resistance. By being in resistance, you are not in your power of creation. Instead you are activating that which you are resisting. The scientific reason for this is; energy flows to where your attention goes. So if you think thoughts like, "I don't want to get sick" and you feel fear about getting sick, you are focused on sickness. Guess what comes next? If you are thinking thoughts like, "I feel broke" then the attention is on that broke energy and before you know it, things will start breaking and you will have more reasons to feel broke.

So it's important to acknowledge where you are on those subjects that you would like to shift from. Do this by quieting your mind and asking within what the feelings, beliefs and emotions are around the subject and why you are feeling that way.

You can no longer be in denial if you want to shift the energy around the subject. By going within and acknowledging your feelings you have the ability to then ask them to be released and to create a whole new awareness around them so you can choose to focus upon what you really want.

As you release those low level old belief systems, you now have the power to create something more in alignment with what you are looking to identify with. Ask within how you want to feel about this subject and intend or decide that you will begin activating the identity of those belief systems. Here is a great example:

Old Belief System

I don't like my job and I feel imprisoned by having to go to a place every day that I absolutely hate.

New Belief System

I know that my current job is creating a strong desire in me for a new opportunity that feels more in alignment with my passion and joy. Every time something happens now at work, I see it as "nails in the coffin" to an experience that no longer aligns with my new identity.

I know that it takes the physical a little more time than the energetic world to manifest what I am wanting so I just need to look for things I like in my current situation. I just need to look for reasons to feel satisfied and know that in my satisfied state a very satisfying opportunity is being activated.

Manifestion complete.

Best friends 32 years and counting. Goldyn Duffy and Michael Duffy

Duffy tribe. Shaelinn, Emma, Goldyn, Michael, Kaylee, Jade

Chasing the sunset in California.

Kinsley Jane, the best thing ever.

Jade and Casey. Happily ever after. Enjoying life in Southern California.

Seriously my baby has the cutest baby.

Nails in the coffin in Connecticut. Dude where's my car?

Back in Connecticut raising 4 girls.

7

MINDFUL AND AWARE

Now your job is to become super aware and interrupt the thought patterns that bring you back to a low level vibration. The best way to do this is to become mindful and present in your everyday life. Becoming present means you are bringing your entire self to experiences and no longer having the negative commentary that has accompanied your activities up until now.

By clearing your mind and staying present, you will deactivate the thought patterns that have been creating your experience. You will pull your attention away from those things that you no longer wish to create.

It is important to explain momentum right here and right now. Understand that you have been thinking the same thoughts day in and day out for as long as you have been alive. Your life experience has caused you to make certain judgments and perceptions that have created the life that you are now living. It is possible to bring forth big changes fast but it is also important to recognize that creating a new momentum is going to take focus and work. Not work, meaning hard work that you have to punch a time clock for, but instead mental work that you are going to need to strengthen over time.

As you practice quieting your mind and focusing on what is in front of you, you will get better and better at doing it. The mind is a very busy bee that will keep dragging you back time and time again, so be aware and also very forgiving of yourself, each time you catch yourself in the craziness of mind banter.

I have spoken with many people who tell me it is not possible for them to quiet their mind or that they cannot meditate because their mind is too busy. This is a belief system that will kill your practice. We all have the ability to come back to zero state awareness: it is who we are and it is what we are infinitely connected to. Release any of the BS your mind is telling you and recognize that in order to get good at something, you must first be bad at it. In order to get really good at something, you have to give it time and attention and lots of practice.

8

SATISFACTION

If you have been living in a state of dissatisfaction, it is time for you to start redirecting your thoughts to more things that satisfy you. Whenever you are feeling dissatisfied, it means that you are pointed in the direction of what you don't want and moving away from the happiness and joy that could be your life. You are taking life for granted and missing out on the amazing opportunities life is giving you to feel satisfied.

When you decide that you will start looking for reasons to feel satisfied and stop at nothing to conjure up the vibrational resonance with those things that feel good, you will point yourself in the direction of all that you are wanting. You will create a flow in the Universe towards wonderful things that feel satisfying to you.

I have heard the word grateful used and overused. Sometimes it's a struggle to feel gratitude especially when you are facing things in your day that you are definitely NOT grateful for. That's why the word and feeling of satisfaction works so much better. It will tune you into better feeling thoughts and doesn't insist that you make the jump from misery to gratitude, which can often feel like too much. Once you start to send out the signal of satisfaction, the Universe picks up on that and gives you more and more reasons to feel satisfied. And if your not careful you may just end up feeling grateful!

Make a list of thoughts and subjects in your life right now that feel satisfying to you. Decide that you will add to this list everyday until you wake up in the morning and this has become a habit.

9

NEURAL PATHWAYS

It's time to get a little technical so you can understand how your brain works and why you have these patterns of thoughts that you may feel are literally "thinking you." You may even be thinking right now that it's not possible to gain control of this crazy mind of yours because it has been running wild for so long. This is why I'm including this next part so you can get a visual and appease your logical mind.

Imagine there are pathways in your brain, well worn pathways that have been thinking the same thoughts for a long, long time. You have created belief systems that support these thoughts and you continue day in and day out to think and believe them. You have set up a vibrational resonance that is bringing you exactly what you are thinking and believing. Most people do not even realize this is happening and that is why we can often feel like our mind cannot be controlled. Along with these patterns of thought, you have created a momentum in your life that proves over and over again that your thoughts and beliefs are in fact correct. Your life is evidence of what you are resonating with.

Here is a new belief system for you. YOU ARE NOT YOUR MIND. What?! I know, right? Your mind is probably telling you that I'm crazy right now and that can't possibly be true. But it is. I know. How, you ask? Because I have separated myself from my mind and discovered a whole new person inside. I have discovered the truth of who I am and that there are many things that I am good at and have the ability to accomplish that I used to think I couldn't do.

This is probably one of the most fascinating discoveries and the most life changing information that I have ever stumbled upon.

Throughout your life you have had experiences and influential people guiding you and helping you to create the beliefs and judgments you have about everything that is going on or has gone on around you. Because of your experiences, you will have certain reactions and judgments to things and you will view life a certain way. This has caused major limitation in your life and created a subconscious vibrational resonance with things that you may not want to be creating.

It's time to recognize that your thoughts are not you. Your thoughts are just a product of things you have experienced and patterns of thoughts that you believed you had no control over. Until now.

So who are you then?

You are pure positive energy that is connected to the stream of All That Is. You have access to Infinite Intelligence any time you quiet your mind and invite It in. You are here to discover that you are an unlimited being with infinite potential and because you are reading this book, it is time for you to step fully into your truth.

Whoa. I know. Too much or are you resonating?

On some level your real knowing is jumping up and down and so excited that you are still reading this.

Or maybe it's time to breathe. Go back into your body. Allow yourself to resonate with what you just read. It's huge, I know. But it's the truth and as soon as you spend more time getting to know yourself on the inside, you will understand this at a whole new level.

Can you imagine what the world would be like if we all walked around with this knowing? If we all let go of unworthiness and our beliefs about lack and limitation? If we all stepped off the merry go round and stopped making a big deal about the shit that just doesn't matter and instead started living from our greatest potential. That's the world I'm interested in. That's the reason I am writing this book and sitting outside on a beautiful Southern California day and telling you that it is possible. Not only is it possible but the tides are already turning in your favor as you take all of this in. As we awaken the truth within ourselves, we begin experiencing life at a whole new level.

This may seem like a lot to ingest, especially if you have just begun this journey of deliberate creation. I promise it will get easier with time and the more you can tune yourself to the quiet within, the more this truth will become your own.

In fact, if this seems too much for you, I'm going to suggest that you put this book down. Yup don't even finish it and spend the next 30 days practicing quieting your mind. Then after 30 days come back and read this all over again and see if the truth resonates more.

THE MOTHER OF ALL MANIFESTATION STORIES

I've lived in Connecticut my entire life and have always had a desire to move to California. I have no idea (well maybe I do) where and when this idea started within me but around age 40 it started to get seriously loud. Possibly due to the fact that I was meditating regularly and getting really good at listening to my intuition. My husband, Michael, had also grown up in Connecticut and had built a pretty successful remodeling construction business that afforded us to buy a home and nice cars and take care of our family of four girls.

We lived in what I used to call my forever home. It was a 5 bedroom, dutch colonial with a wrap around front porch, a huge level yard, a pool and a hot tub. I won't bore you with the detail of the miracle of finding our home but I will say that I was deliberately creating before I even knew it. So we began our journey, raising our family as my husband was building his business. Life had it's happy moments but looking back I can see how incredibly stressed we were. We had teenagers and toddlers and a very busy schedule. My husband's business was thriving, but he was super stressed and extremely busy. We spent money like crazy to help us feel better about the stress, and alcohol was definitely used on a daily basis to help deal with everything.

I can see now that those were happy times but times in which we had no idea how we were creating or what energy we were conducting. I remember feeling anxious a lot when I spent money but it didn't seem to stop me because I was just trying to feel better. We went to church every Sunday and taught the girls about God. We prayed and read the Bible. We took part in Bible Studies and retreats. My intuitive connection started when I would lead guided meditations to the different women's groups I was a part of. My prayers were not meditative, but instead pleas to God to help me with parenting the girls and whatever else I was worried about.

In 2008 when the economy crashed, our business went down with it. We faced financial ruin, foreclosure on our home and car repossessions. Miracle upon miracle happened at this time but that's another book for another time.

I can see now how that experience lead us to the desires we began to pursue and fulfill. There was so much growth and faith that was built during this time. I believe it gave us the courage to do what my heart was calling us to do.

Yeah, that's right. Michael wasn't quite on board to move across the country to a place he had only visited for one day. In fact, when we visited California on our layover to Hawaii a year before, it actually rained and my husband said, " I don't think I even like it here." Dammit.

The funny thing about desire is that if it is something you are meant to do, it will never fully go away. You can push it down for years and try to ignore it, but the reality is you will just get more and more miserable in what you are living. Your desire will continue to call you and in each passing year it will get stronger and stronger. Our desires get stronger by the contrast that we live and the ideas of our desire will begin to show up at every turn. This is what happened to me, no matter how much I tried to be ok with where I was, my heart was crying out for more.

It was at this time that we discovered Universal Law and started to put into practice much of what I am writing about here. Our lives started to change rapidly and we were seeing miracles on a daily basis.

During a business event for a new business venture we were involved with, I bumped into a gentleman who was from Southern California. I told him that I really wanted to live there and my husband, who was so not interested at the time, walked away. This man told me that if I ever wanted to know anything about living in SoCal, he was the guy to ask. I remember feeling so much hope and a lot of wishing. I know now that I was living in the lack of it and still wondering if it could ever really happen. Little did I know that one year later, we would embark on the journey of a lifetime.

The entire process of creating this strong desire to moving across the country, took me four years. I can see how I slowed down the energy, but was also readying myself for the move. I could feel the lack I felt and began shifting it with intense meditation and a deep appreciation for where I was. I knew that California was a high vibe place and if I was feeling depressed and hating where I was, I would never get there.

Our manifestation powers come from our ability to get in the receiving mode. If you are walking around and hating where you are in life, you are not in the receiving mode. When you quiet your mind, relax your being, and find ways to feel more satisfied, you activate the energy of allowing. By finding reasons to feel joy you put yourself in the most powerful, manifestational energy there is.

I made the decision even though I knew I didn't quite have my man on board yet. For those four years, I vacillated between being excited about moving to California and feeling the major lack that I wasn't there yet. I acted in faith and even threw out all of our winter stuff one year to unfortunately, face another cold New England winter and having to buy new stuff. I meditated like my life depended on it. I set intentions and wrote them down constantly.

To be honest, I didn't even know what it was really like to live in California. I just knew I belonged there. Sometimes this happens in life, where we have a strong calling to a place or an experience that doesn't make a whole lot of sense. When we are tuned in to our internal voice, we begin to follow those callings with a knowing that even though it may not have been in your life plan, that the calling is worth listening to.

Then an interesting thing happened. Michael, who isn't one to spend time on studying spirituality, actually paid for a session with an energy healer we had met on Facebook who lived in Germany. I was so fascinated by his session with her that I booked one as well.

Over the next few months we created a relationship with this woman and became really clear on what we wanted to create in our lives. We both came to the definite decision that we wanted to live in Southern

California and so it really began to form.

We got super clear over that summer. Started visualizing and meditating to the sounds of the ocean, talking about it and getting super excited. We started seeing signs everywhere constantly and we kept seeing that as encouragement to keep moving towards our dream. One day, when I was doing some business in upstate New York, I saw 7 California license plates! I knew that I was getting closer with my vibrational alignment and every sign I saw only confirmed that.

I then got an intuitive message that I should contact the man I saw at the business event and see if he could give me any information on the best place to live. I had no contact information but I knew his name and thankfully I found him on Facebook. Once I sent him a friend request, he messaged me right back and asked me if I was trying to get a hold of him. We started having regular phone calls and one day he said to me, "You have to come out here. You can't possibly move without visiting first." He said we could stay with him and a friend of his would show us all around Southern California. I got really excited and set the intentions.

Soon after, I won the lottery for $928. We decided that this was a sign and we booked a scouting trip for 8 days throughout Southern California. We thought that once we were here we could make connections for work and then when we moved, we would be all set. This was the first week of September and my intention was to be moved before winter started again in New England. We had the absolute time of our lives. I remember sitting on a picnic table in Laguna Beach, California thinking, "Could this really be my home?" I now live ten minutes from there. In my opinion, it's one of the most beautiful places in the country.

Just writing this brings tears to my eyes. It is such a wonderful feeling being on the other side of this incredible manifestation. To sit at that picnic table now and feel so at home brings me so much satisfaction. It has truly made all the ups and downs so worth it. When you finally realize your dream, something you have dreamed about for a long time, it gives you a great feeling of confidence and an intense feeling of the power you have to create. This is my vibrational set point now. I know there is nothing I can't be, do or have.

After our trip, nothing happened. No connections except for the woman who was our businessman's friend. She and I would talk from time to time and she would list out possible places that we could live. I had no idea at this time how it was going to happen I just knew in my heart that it was just a matter of time.

That winter, I decided that I needed to stop being miserable. I knew California had a high vibe and I knew if I was miserable getting through winter, I would not line up with the energy of California. So I decided to be happy no matter what the weather would bring. Every time it snowed and I found myself shoveling, I would put on some great music and dance through it. I felt like it was "nails in the coffin" and every storm just brought me closer to realizing my dream.

Financially, Michael's business was doing well and we were starting to feel more abundant. At the time, our house had been in foreclosure for five years and the banks would not allow us to come out of it until we paid $100,000. Even though we had the money to pay our mortgage, they would not allow us to do that. We went to court over the course of those years and every time, they kept letting us live in our house. Now I don't recommend this, but I will say it is an absolute freaking miracle that we manifested staying as long as we did. I could see in my mind's eye, paperwork being shuffled and our house always being put at the bottom of the pile.

In February, we got a letter from the bank that we had a court date that we thought was about the bank taking back our home. We decided at that moment that we needed to make a definite decision and a leap of faith. I told Michael that the house would not be taken from us. I felt strong in my knowing that we would give the house back when we were ready. I felt a huge wave of energy when I said, "Why are we waiting for the bank to determine our fate?"

Even though I was excited to have this conversation with my husband and make these huge decisions and plans, I remember feeling very terrified. When we aim to jump high, there are so many factors that can cause boatloads of fear within us. The secret to mastering the fear is to keep moving forward in faith and allow your desire to drive so fast that your fear has no chance of slowing you down.

So we acted in total faith. We put a date on our move for the week after the kids ended school in June. We set an intention to have $30,000 to move to California. We booked plane tickets for the four of us and our two cats (our oldest daughter was already living on her own in CT and would hopefully join us later, and our second daughter was already living in Arizona).

We started to tell the girls and they were excited about it. I think it helped that it was the middle of winter and we talked about sunshine and beaches. I think they were feeding off of our excitement but would find it really hard to leave the only home they knew and all of their friends. Their excitement helped us to feel even better about our decision and to catapult our plans forward.

At one point in April, we had a court date on the house and I attended it because I wanted to make sure they would let us stay until our flights left. The judge looked at me and said, "Ma'am there is no sale date for your house." It would be six months after we left before they would do anything with our house! I believe it was my very strong intention that I would give back the house and that it would never be taken from me that created this outcome.

The next few months were an absolute whirlwind. When you leap in faith, the Universe meets you in the most incredible and fascinating ways. Michael started getting really abundant opportunities, and I started selling everything we owned. I began cleaning out the house we had lived in with our family for the last ten years. Every day brought more money in and a feeling of excitement that is hard to describe. We did not tell anyone our plans for a while because we were not interested in anyone telling us why it was a crazy idea.

When you decide to follow your dreams and do crazy shit, people around you may not be supportive. They will give you every reason why their life experience has told them that it's a bad idea. When Michael told the guy he was doing his last job for that he was moving to Southern California, this old yankee said, "What the hell are you moving there for? There's a bunch of weirdos out there."

Setting out to do something that may appear crazy, is not for the weak. In fact, I would highly advise that you do not tell anyone what you are planning, unless you want to introduce their resistance around it. Everyone has an opinion, and their opinions are based on their life experience. They do not have this crazy desire burning through them and calling them to more, or do they? People also do not like to see others change their lives, because it means that they may not be pursuing the dreams they have been called to. It shines a spotlight on the inner callings that they have shushed in order to keep life complacent, and trapped in a life that feels safe.

I wish I could tell you that we knew what we were doing but we really didn't. Sometimes when you follow your inner guidance, you will do things that just don't make sense. The guys that Michael knew couldn't fathom why he would leave a thriving business to move to the unknown. A place where he didn't know the building laws or even how to build for earthquakes. I am one lucky girl to be married to someone who knows who he is and what he is capable of. My husband has a strong drive and a knowing that he is capable of massive success no matter where he is. He took on the belief some time ago that he would always have work and always create abundance. It was this belief that he took with him to California and in a few short years he would create exactly what he set out for.

Boarding the plane on June 30 was one of the scariest, saddest, most exciting times of our lives. I remember feeling wracked with anxiety and the pain of leaving our oldest daughter in Connecticut. At the time, she was engaged to a man who we knew would never move to California. Leaving the only home you have ever known and every person you have connection to is not for the weak. We had no idea where we would find a home or job. At this point, we were acting on total faith and trust that our dreams would be realized.

When you allow a desire to drive you, there is no turning back in fear. The key is to keep going, keep planning, and keep moving forward, despite the fears. Create such a strong determination and decision that nothing can derail you from what you deserve to be living. Were there times when we felt we had made a mistake? Absolutely. Were there times when we felt tons of fear and kept going? Definitely. But at some point, we made the decision that we had come too far to fail. That we had to keep going because going back felt like death. We kept each other going and picked each other up when the other was down. Our family became a true team and we saw each other through some very uncertain and scary times. There is no doubt we are all stronger and better for it.

One of the very first extremely cool manifestations we had was a friend of ours that we lost touch with, reconnected with us when she found out we were moving. She was one of the 3 people we knew in California and it turned out that she was leaving for Hawaii the same day we were flying in and offered us her beautiful home to stay in. We told her we could take her car home from the airport so she wouldn't have to pay to leave it there. We also offered to watch her dog. This way we had 10 days to find a home and wouldn't have to pay for a hotel. Our car wasn't due to arrive for four more days so this was an incredibly helpful manifestation to be able to use her car to find our new home.

For the next week, we worked on acclimating to this new state and getting our bearings on where we might want to live. My friend that had showed us around the first time gave me a bunch of towns that might interest us, so we began checking them out. We had no idea how much we could spend having no income at the time and the rent felt really high. We also had very low credit scores because of all the financial stuff we had gone through. These were definitely mountains we needed to move. I remember sitting with a real estate agent who was showing us houses that were absolutely awful. He was telling us we were going to have to settle for a crappy house until we could build up our credit and establish income. I remember getting really mad in his office. I remember thinking, "this guy has no idea who we are and how we create."

We left the real estate office feeling very determined and slightly pissed off. The wonderful thing about anger is that it can be very productive when it puts you in a state of action and determination.

We branched out on our own and started looking online for places. We met up with a wonderful woman down in San Clemente who had a rental that was not right for us but helped us to see and feel the energy of the town. I didn't feel quite right there, but kept following the energy of where we were being called.

We decided to go look at another rental in San Clemente and on the way there we needed to stop for gas. We got off an exit in a town called Aliso Viejo. Once we got off the highway something happened. It was the first place that felt really good to me. I looked around at the town center with it's movie theater and stores and thought, "Whoa, I could live here." There was something about the town that felt good. It felt safe and welcoming. After we got gas, we headed back to San Clemente to a rental that was in a gas station parking lot. We didn't even go in.

The next day I received an email from an apartment complex in Aliso Viejo. I couldn't believe it!! We called and scheduled an appointment that day. After walking through the model unit (that was a 3 bedroom 1700 square foot apartment) visiting the four pools, hot tubs and the gym, we got very excited. It felt like a resort! Now being country folk, we had never considered this type of "condensed living" but the place felt so good to us and we knew we had to start somewhere. We put in our application and prayed that they would accept us, despite our credit scores.

By that time, our stay in our friends house had ended and we were now staying in a hotel. At $250 a night, and some very close quarters, the tension was pretty high. It was like sitting on pins and needles in that hotel, waiting for them to get back to us over a very, very long weekend. The girls were not happy and we were feeling super stressed about the fact that we were homeless and scared. Deep, deep down in our hearts, we knew everything always worked out for us, but this was a whole new level of faith being called forth.

After we survived the weekend, the apartment complex told us that we would only need $400 extra in our deposit to make up for the bad credit scores. I can't even express to you the type of relief I felt that we were no longer homeless and we were moving to a place that felt safe and beautiful. It was happening. Things were continuing to work out for us.

We had to wait about ten more days before we could move in because we wanted a corner unit. This meant more light and no neighbors on one side of our unit. Those ten days were not fantastic. We were in a small two bedroom hotel with two adolescents who were at each other constantly. We had no privacy and our cats were slightly terrified after being in a kitty hotel for the last week.

Moving in was easy because we didn't really have any furniture. We had to go bed shopping and spend a lot of money on furniture that was very pricey. I decided to take out furniture credit cards that had no financing for two years to help us reserve some of our funds. This turned out to be a very smart thing that helped us build our credit back up. We ordered a couch but had to sit on beach chairs until it was delivered for the first few weeks. Our coffee table was a cardboard box that the new vacuum came in. And we lived without much else until we could build back up again. It was ok to go without. I had made a decision that I would only surround myself with things that I absolutely love and I would patiently manifest and fill in the holes with furniture that felt right.

Money was going out super fast as we were getting the necessities. Since we only brought what we could fit in my car, there were a lot of things we needed. And with tons of money going out and no money coming in, the fear started to become palpable.

We ended up needing to get a truck for Michael because the truck he had in CT was sent to the junkyard just before we left. We went to a car dealership, put the truck in my name and had no idea how we would make the payments. I can see how much we were acting in faith and just trusting that it was all going to work out for us. Not for the weak.

Michael is one who responds to fear by getting into action. He knew he had to do something to get money flowing in, so he took a job in LA from a lead we had gotten from a friend in CT. The guys he started working for loved him but couldn't pay him more than $35/hour. He was driving in traffic for about 5 hours a day for a wage that did not even come close to paying the rent. He did this for four days and then had a talk with the guys he was working for. They offered to put him up in a hotel for 4 days a week and pay him a little more. Even though this was an opportunity to make some money, we both decided that we didn't move to California to be away from each other four days a week. He let the job go. This kind of terrified me, I'm not gonna lie.

It's important to understand that we are always at choice. It is easy for us to work from fear and do things to make money when we feel there may be no other alternative. This is the deal; there is always another alternative. There is always ways in which we will be supported when we say no to the things that are simply not working for us. There is always another opportunity right around the corner waiting for you to let go of the one that is not working. My husband is very good at this and I have seen him manifest some amazing opportunities by not holding onto things out of desperation and fear.

That Sunday we had a coffee date planned with a couple we had never met before but were friends with on Facebook. They saw our post on Facebook, that we had moved into the area and they loved that we had followed our dreams. We had a wonderful conversation with these folks during which they told us about a networking group they were involved in. There was a gentleman in the group who did high end remodels in the area and our new friends would talk to him and see if he needed any help.

Turns out he did. I love the Universe.

Over the next few months, Michael worked for Bob and Karen. They were so good to us and paid us as much as they could. They also included a stipend to pay our truck payment every month. (Remember that truck payment that I didn't know how we were going to pay?) Boom. When I say Bob and Karen were angels, I'm not kidding. A few weeks into working, Michael was feeling frustrated because all of his tools were back in CT. We had plans to go back and get them when we were all settled and had a place to put them. Bob offered to loan us money so that Michael could go back, rent a truck and bring his tools home. Bob and Karen helped us through one of the scariest times of our lives and provided us with the information and financial support to begin creating our own abundance.

The Universe will send you angels and support in many ways. When you act in faith, there is no end to the support you will receive. It's ok if you have fear as long as you continue to move forward and listen to your inner guidance. We thought of that coffee date as a clue to what may be coming next and sure enough it was. If we had stayed home in fear and misery, we would have missed out on this amazing opportunity that saw us through until the next amazing thing happened.

During this time, my business started to really pick up. Back in CT, I was doing speaking engagements on Universal Law and coaching private clients through different experiences they wanted help with. When I moved to California, I tapped into an ability that helped others to release the energy and belief systems that were holding them back. I began to discover their low level belief systems that had been created long ago and were still creating in their life. I began doing energy releasing and helped my clients to heal from a lifetime of wounds. I found my channel to the Divine and began a coaching business that perfectly unfolded. To this day, I have never looked for clients, nor advertised. Word of mouth got out and I was able to pull in miraculous income to help sustain us at this time. This further grew my faith and enhanced my gifts and knowledge of how the Universe works.

Going through challenging times is a huge part of our expansion and growth. We are called to find our strength and power within. Challenges create a strong foundation of faith and we can always come out better for it, if you can find the gifts in your experience. I know that this time of extreme financial uncertainty is part of my work and part of what I am helping heal in others. The amount of compassion and understanding I can now offer to others is exponential since going through all of that. Everything we go through is for great purpose. I know that what I went through is part of instilling the faith and confidence in others to know that it's gonna be okay.

Our challenges call more life through us. The reason for this is when we experience contrasting experiences, we develop more capacity for joy. You really don't know how good something feels until you experience what it's like to not have it. I have never appreciated a full tank of gas the way I do now, after not having enough money at times to fill my tank. Talk to anyone who has had a serious illness and they will tell you they no longer sweat the small stuff. They now experience a whole new appreciation for life because the threat of losing their life gave them perspective.

So many miracles and manifestations happened through these six months. We would have money come in from the most unexpected places. I believe this was to expand our faith and trust that we would always be supported in pursuing our dreams. We would visit the ocean when we felt extreme fear and let the waves tell us that we lived in an abundant Universe. When you visit the ocean and tune into the never ending energy and abundance it has to offer, your entire spirit feels better for it. It always provides us with a knowing that our well being is always supported. We allowed the ocean waves to wash away our fears and remind us of why we had followed our dreams. It soothed us into a calming state of mind which always helped us get back into receiving mode.

On days where we would feel heavy about our situation, we would go chase the sunset because that was always reassuring. We could always count on the sun to set and it made us aware that we could always count on tomorrow to show us more miracles. It was imperative for us to quiet our mind and tune into the frequency of nature. There are so many miracles happening around us on a daily basis and things that we can count on to provide us with hope and faith. Whenever you are faced with the seriousness of life feeling too heavy, I highly recommend a good dose of the sunset, sunrise or the ocean waves to bring you back to the love and support that is available to you when you look up from all your challenges.

CHRISTMAS MANIFESTION

Right before our very first California Christmas, we had an issue with one of Bob's checks. The girl in the office put it in the mail on Friday and Christmas was on Saturday. Michael was hoping to pick it up because we had NO money. Before the panic could even set in, we went to the mailbox and had received a check from our old mortgage company, you know the one that foreclosed on our house. They sent us $2000!! We call this mailbox money! We felt so incredibly blessed. It felt like a Christmas miracle! Without it, we would not have had a Christmas that year. This was an especially heavy holiday because we were no longer around family.

Throughout this whole process we learned how to feel happy no matter what our bank account said. We did things that didn't cost money and we became closer and stronger as a family. Whenever an unexpected expense would show up, **we felt into our complete faith** that all things were always working out for us and before we knew it the money would show up.

When we go through uncertain times it is easy to get swallowed by fear and darkness. Our old programming of not having enough or feeling unworthy of abundance can kick up at any time if you have not healed it. If you can resist the urge to let the fear take you out and make you miserable you will create more favored outcomes faster. If you dive deep into allowing and believing it's always working out for you, your faith will expand and you will tap into infinite miracles. I am forever grateful for the times that have shown me just how powerful we are. They have been a springboard to all I teach and to the compassion I am now able to offer.

After just a few short years of intending, we are now in a place of abundance. Once we set our intentions to create a thriving business the work came in and continues to astound and delight us. We worked on lining ourselves up with what we know we are worthy and capable of, and the excitement for more can always be felt. We are living examples of aligning energy with abundance and reaping the benefits of releasing fears and limitations. Our lives are unfolding quite magically and we continue to live in a state of positive expectations and deep satisfaction.

Even though things were working out so well for us, we had this underlying desire to have all of our daughters living in California.

I had mentioned earlier that my eldest daughter stayed back in CT because she was engaged to someone who did not want to move to California. Our hope was that we would have them visit in the winter and he would be hooked. No such luck. He was not a fan of sunshine. Huh? He was fair skinned and seemed insulted that the sun was shining all the time here! So it looked as though my dream of our family all living out West might not come true. Luckily, I know better and I know that focusing on the alignment of things is how to manifest.

I decided that I would spend no time missing her and I wouldn't feel angst that she wasn't living near us. I accepted the fact that she was living what was right for her and that I had no idea how she would end up living in California, I just knew that she would.

If it appears as though things are not working towards the fulfillment of your desires, hang tight. Stay focused on what you want and do your best not to try to convince anyone to do what you want them to do. Soon enough your energetic alignment with what you want will deliver in the most surprising way.

About a year after we left, we received a phone call from our daughter hysterically crying that her relationship had ended. We felt incredibly helpless being so many miles away and not being able to console her. We talked for a while and decided that we would come back in a month and move her out to California.

Our hearts were broken for her. This was a five year relationship to someone she truly loved. Michael and I went through so much heartache for her and felt tortured that we couldn't be with her at this difficult time. We talked on the phone every day and did the best we could to support her through her heartbreak. We vacillated between the anguish of her situation and the excitement of having our family together again.

We could have never imagined that this would happen the way that it did. Often times we can't see how things will work out so we just have to know they will and move forward in faith.

A few days before we were going to move her to California, I received a call from my second daughter with some news. She told me that my oldest daughter was already in a new relationship with the guy that she had been working with. I was shocked. I knew that he had not left her side since the break up and I kind of felt sorry for him, thinking he must be in love with her. He is quite a bit older than her so I didn't think anything was going on between them. Turns out they fell in love and the plan was that he would move out to California with her six months later.

One of the most amazing things about this is seeing my daughter so happy. I love seeing her with someone who loves her for who she is and only wants to create happiness with her. That first relationship would have never helped her to find the joy that she lives today and as I see them together, I know that they were so meant to be together. I'm happy to say they are now engaged to be married.

So now my entire family is on the West Coast. I could have never imagined it would work out the way that it did, but I do know that everything is always working out for me.

10

RECEIVING MODE

Things happen in life that create a desire within you. You then look for physical ways to bring them to fruition. The practice has been to use your physical experience to work hard and struggle to bring things into your life. Once you begin to quiet your mind, you will activate another level of thinking and you will start to create more easily. You will begin to understand that energetic alignment is way more effective than physical struggle and way more fun.

As you exercise your right to invite in the Universe to help you create things, you will activate so much more potential in your experience. There are energies and fields that you do not even have awareness of until you begin to quiet your mind. There are other levels to your brain and manifestation powers that you have not even scratched the surface of.

By quieting your mind you will stop the thoughts that have been keeping you in lackful, low vibrational thinking. You will allow enough space and a calming to your momentum that will allow new energies to transcribe. When you relax, you put yourself in the receiving mode. You see, when you worry and wait for things, you actually slow the energy to create them way down. When you shift the way you have been thinking about them and begin to call upon the Universal partnership to assist, you will see very different results.

It's ok to ask for what you want, but realize that if you keep asking (which means worrying, waiting, asking where it is) you are not in receiving mode. You slow down the quantum energy that you are working on amping up every time you notice or worry that you haven't manifested that thing yet. When we feel as if we are deprived of something we are in energetic alignment of it's absence.

Get in the receiving mode by allowing the physical energy to catch up with the energetic world. This means relaxing more and worrying never.

11

IT'S SCIENCE, BABY

If you can imagine that when you have a desire, you send out a quantum wave of energy that breaks down into particles and becomes matter, you might be able to relax more. If you can wrap your mind around the fact that everything is energy and we are powerful conductors of energy, then you will ignite your power. Understand that all of your desires are dripping with the potential to manifest. In fact, they are more likely than not, in the process of becoming part of your experience. Especially after reading this book.

The reason why many things don't manifest in your experience is because of your inability to focus. Most of the time we will decide we want something and then change our mind again and again depending on what we believe is possible. Remember me and my Mercedes? It didn't actually break that wave into particles until I became super focused for a very short time. I energetically aligned myself and knew that it was coming.

So remember if you are working on something and it hasn't come yet, your only job is to quiet your mind about it and begin creating the identity that allows you to align with it.

12

IT'S TIME TO REALIZE
YOUR DREAMS

You are in a great position right now, possibly more than ever before, to bring the energetic into physical form. You now have the tools and the steps to allow yourself to align with whatever it is that you have been wanting. Understand that if you have made broad statements like, "I just wanna be rich," you won't have much manifestation power behind that.

Ask yourself what you really want to feel and then decide that your life will begin to reflect that. Begin activating those feelings wherever and whenever you can. If it's financial riches you are after, ask yourself, "what does abundance feel like to me?" or "how can I notice more abundance in my life?"

If it's a life partner you are looking for, then find ways to no longer feel lonely or feel that you are lacking something. Use this time to get to know and love yourself better so that when that partner does show up he/she will be the perfect reflection of the beautiful, healed, whole person you have focused on becoming.

Whatever it is that you are looking to manifest, it's time to ask yourself and get real clear about what that looks and feels like. For way too long, you have been living in the lack of what you have been wanting. Once you shift your energy and belief about it, you will experience quantum leaps like never before. This is what happens when we begin aligning our energetic world with what we want, it is quantum leaping at it's finest.

Here are the steps to clearly define your manifestational powers:

Decide that you are creating what you want

Quiet your mind to release old momentums-refer to my website for guidance, www.goldynduffy.com

Release any resistance or thoughts that are in the opposite direction of what you want

Invite in the co-creative partnership of the Universe

Identify with your new identity

Exercise your right to feel excitement and joy

Know this: the feeling is the manifestation. Once things have manifested we tend to move onto something else. Enjoy the journey, take stock in your current abilities, and appreciate the hell out of the fact that you have been brought here to live your fullest most powerful life experience.

Also: the mere fact that you have a desire means you have what it takes to manifest it, otherwise you would not have that desire present in your awareness. Begin to have confidence in your manifestational powers and know that you are on this journey for great purpose.

Enjoy the journey more. As you begin to focus on things that satisfy you more and decide that you will spend time with those things that make you feel good, your life will start to uplevel.

As you focus on the good, more good will come.

Before you know it your life will be the exact reflection of all that you knew it could be and more.

Happy Creating!

If you are feeling like you could really use support on this journey I highly recommend you join the M21 Revolution. This is a private facebook group that presents a 21 day challenge that assists you with guided meditations, mind training, and videos that help you to understand Universal Law at it's core. We are an expanding, leading edge group of change makers taking thought beyond what it's been before. You can join anytime and have access to life changing Universal knowledge. Here's the link to join www.goldynduffy.com/ m21-revolution.

13

FINAL THOUGHTS

Pay attention to the signs from the Universe.

Your soul already knows where you are going.

Pay attention to the things that light you up.

Pay attention to the subtle signs and "coincidences" that can easily be missed when we are too worried about trying to figure out "how" things are going to happen.

The how is not your job.

The how will unfold miraculously and delight you in many ways. It is beyond your thinking mind.

YOUR SOUL ALREADY KNOWS WHERE IT'S GOING

A few years before we moved to California, Michael googled images of Southern California and saved a photo to his wallpaper on his phone. The idea was that every time he would look at his phone it would activate the desire within him to live in the beauty of Southern California.

Shortly after we moved to California, we felt inspired to go to a yoga meetup group overlooking the ocean. We were both feeling pretty anxious and needed to ground and calm ourselves in some way. The funny thing is, Michael was never interested in yoga, so when he mentioned it to me I was delighted.

We arrived a few minutes early and decided to take a walk and look at the ocean. As we looked out we became astounded by the fact that we were looking out at the exact view of the picture from Michael's phone that he had found on Google years before. He always said that we would live near that scene and now we were.

We both started to cry.

Your soul already knows where you are going.

This is why meditating is so important to our journeys.

When we quiet the mind we come in contact with our soul.

When we come in contact with our soul, we activate the energy of faith and peace. We activate the energy of not needing to know how it's all going to happen, but instead knowing that it's all going to happen in the most perfect way.

Everything is working out so well for you.
Know it in every fiber of your being.
It is yours to know.

About Goldyn Duffy

Goldyn Duffy is a Universal Law, meditation and mindfulness educator. She is a speaker, author, and co-founder of the M21 Revolution, an online collective of leading-edge change makers.

It was over two decades ago that she showed up frazzled to a playgroup with her toddlers. Mother to four girls, the other two being teenagers at the time, left her challenged in ways she could have never imagined. She noticed a friend that morning that was living the calm that she craved and it was from here that she was led to the practice of meditation. It was that very day that she set herself on a trajectory towards a life of healing and deliberate creation. With the addition of meditation in her life she was able to tap into patience she never knew she had before. From this patience, her relationship with her husband and daughters deepened. Her life became clearer and her freedom to choose was unveiled.

In 2008, Goldyn and her husband watched as their multi-million dollar business dissolved leaving them with a home in foreclosure and more motivation than ever to create the life they dreamed of. In addition to her daily meditation practice, she began to study Law of Attraction. She learned how energy works and formulated processes to create real change in her life. These practices led her to follow an intuitive calling to move her family to California from Connecticut. Despite initial resistance from her family, Goldyn stayed focused on her heart's calling. She watched patiently as the resistance fell away allowing everyone to come on board as the plan unfolded.

In 2015, the Duffy's arrived in Southern California.

Not long after the move west, Goldyn unlocked a gift to intuitively access information for others and assist them in moving energy they no longer needed out of their bodies. She has served as a vehicle for change and healing for many people. Thankfully for the rest of the world, she continues to share her wisdom with everyone who crosses her path. Goldyn is the mother to now four beautiful women, wife to her high school sweetheart Michael and "Gigi" to Kinsley Jane. They live in their dream home in Orange County, CA.

Made in the USA
Columbia, SC
22 December 2019